ONCE UPON A DREAM

East Of England

Edited By Emily Johnstone

First published in Great Britain in 2017 by:

YoungWriters Est. 1991

Young Writers
Remus House
Coltsfoot Drive
Peterborough
PE2 9BF
Telephone: 01733 890066
Website: www.youngwriters.co.uk

All Rights Reserved
Book Design by Spencer Hart
© Copyright Contributors 2017
SB ISBN 978-1-78820-456-9
Printed and bound in the UK by BookPrintingUK
Website: www.bookprintinguk.com
YB0333HZ

FOREWORD

Welcome to 'Once Upon a Dream – East Of England'.

For our latest competition for primary school pupils, we were looking for poems inspired by dreams. This could mean the topsy-turvy imaginative world we visit each night, or the aspirations and hopes we have for the future. Some writers also chose to delve into the creepy world of nightmares!

Dreams provide a rich and varied source of inspiration, as is clear from the diverse and entertaining poems we received. It was great to see how the writers had fun with the theme and let their imaginations run riot, as well as getting to grips with poetic forms such as the acrostic. Inside this collection you will find poems about everything from flying to football, with a few vampires and unicorns along the way.

Picking a favourite from the anthology was tough so well done to *Olivia Bushell* who is the winning poet. I would also like to congratulate all the young writers featured in these pages, I hope it encourages you to keep following your writing dreams!

Emily Johnstone

CONTENTS

Winner:

Olivia Bushell (8) - Byfield School, Byfield ... 1

Bozeat Primary School, Bozeat

Libby Betts (9) ... 2
Elize Aimee Lane (10) ... 3
Jemima Rose Denny (8) ... 4
Freyja Clapton (9) ... 5
Isabel Maeve Pellant (9) ... 6
Jazmine Farman (10) ... 7
Sapphire Alison Goodes (10) ... 8
Anya Hillyard (9) ... 9
Finley Repton (9) ... 10
Liam Ross (9) ... 11
Caitlyn Margan (7) ... 12
Myles Jones (10) ... 13

Brackley CE Junior School, Brackley

Hannah Layard (10) ... 14
Samuel Mitchell (11) ... 15
Emily Lawton ... 16
Zsuzsanna Mathe (10) ... 17
Emma Charlotte Rose Williams (10) ... 18

Byfield School, Byfield

Daniel James Clayton (10) ... 19
Rosie Turner (8) ... 20
Chloe Henderson (6) ... 22
Alistair Andrew Smith (8) ... 23
Sebastian Adkins (8) ... 24

Kyran Warne (9) ... 25
Elise Danielle Warne (6) ... 26
Jude O'Connell (9) ... 27
Orla Kate Driscoll (9) ... 28
Sophie Shepherd (9) ... 29
Noah Clarke (7) ... 30
Kayleigh Judge (9) ... 31
Lily Norman ... 32
Jorja Taylor (7) ... 33
Jayden Haynes (6) ... 34
Madison Judge (6) ... 35
Sophie Bushell (7) ... 36
Guy Shepherd (6) ... 37

Fulbourn Primary School, Fulbourn

Matthew Lewis (10) ... 38
Samuel George (11) ... 40
Rosa Grimley Evans (10) ... 42
Dilara Cifci (9) ... 44
Erin Burling (11) ... 45
Libby Jarvis (10) ... 46
Charlie Rickett (10) ... 48
Hanna Stewart ... 49
Logan Neilson (10) ... 50
Mischa Shipton (10) ... 51
Victoria Vireikyte (10) ... 52
Alex Matthew Marson (10) ... 53
Sam Gurney ... 54
Bjorn Ford (10) ... 55
Su-Ad Tungteiya Musah (10) ... 56
Eva Patey (10) ... 57
Bailey James (10) ... 58
Charlie Austwick (10) ... 59
Lisa Distill (11) ... 60

Great Creaton Primary School, Creaton

Holly Carol Rowland (10)	61

Kingsfield Primary School, Chatteris

Isla Draper (10)	62
Phoebe Kate Moore (10)	64
Jamie Toth (10)	66
Ellie Bissett (10)	67
Ryan Fell (10)	68
Rosey Ford (9)	69
Kendra Mae North (10)	70
Wiktoria Julia Drobisz (11)	71
Ellie-Mae Jarvis (10)	72
Olivia Mae Pacey (10)	73
Callum Cooper (10)	74
Evan Harte (10)	75
Jayden Mcdonnell	76
Declan O'Neill (10)	77
Kieran Fisher (10)	78
Jake Singleton (11)	79
Kai Jack Wiltshire (10)	80
Logan Barbault (10)	81
Tegan Smith (11)	82
Lois Wills (10)	83
Ewa Maria Slowik (9)	84
Callum Fitzpatrick (10)	85
Lewie Bond (10)	86
Harry Henman	87
Layla Casey Hobson (10)	88
Jamie Harrington (10)	89

Paulerspury CE Primary School, Paulerspury

Elizabeth Wain (9)	90

Scartho Junior School, Grimsby

Kieran Ames (11)	92
Keira Tupman (11)	93
Jack Brighton (11)	94
Ben Connolly (10)	95
Annas Mohamed (11)	96
Oliver Wiseman (10)	97
Lawrence Jackson (11)	98
Elizabeth Holliday (10)	100
Finlee Robinson (11)	101
Ben Rendall (11)	102

The Arbours Academy, Northampton

Elizabeth Boamah (10)	103
Denroy Welsh (10)	104
Rutendo Mashapa (9)	105
Bartosz Kaczmarczyk (10)	106
Abbie Elizabeth McCallum (10)	107
Aliyah White (10)	108
Dylan Jake Carey (10)	109
Larissa Grimmer (10)	110
Owen Shrubb (10)	111
Reyhana Rahman (10)	112
Stephine Akingbehin (10)	113
Taya Swartz (9)	114
Jason Asante (9)	115
Katy Dempsey (10)	116
Tudor Catrinescu (10)	117

Welton CE Academy, Welton

Grace Lola Sargent (10)	118
India Gries (9)	119
Danny Healey (10)	120
Guy Dawkins (11)	121
Isabella Sophia Dunnett (8)	122
Thomas Carvell (11)	123
Oliver Dunnett (8)	124
Claudia Elizabeth Margaret Cater (10)	125
Issabella Holt (10)	126
Raife O'neill (8)	127
Owen Knox (9)	128
Lucy Nicholls (9)	129
Lily Beatrice Theobald (10)	130
Evie Elizabeth Winn (10)	131

Grace Austin (10)	132
Mimi-Rose Ernest (9)	133
Mia Grace Ainger-Gamble (9)	134
Jessica Souter (9)	135
Matias Rusailh (8)	136
Alexander Paul Cater (9)	137
Erin Middleton (9)	138
Samuel White (10)	139

Wootton St Andrew's Primary School, Wootton

Isabelle Dannatt (8)	140
Isla Grace Turner (9)	141
Joseph Crowe (9)	142
Darcey Siron (8)	144
Jake Nutt (9)	145
Erin O'Mara	146
Thomas Potter (11)	148
Jessica Hutson	149
Jack Clark (9)	150
Amelia Rose Keir (9)	151
Darcey Skelton (10)	152
Esmé Burbidge (8)	153
Oliver Armstrong (10)	154
Lily Dannatt	155
Gracie O'Mara (10)	156
Kurtis Filby (11)	157

THE POEMS

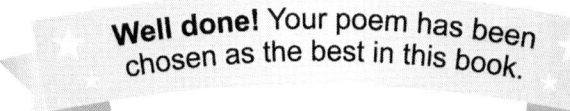

Well done! Your poem has been chosen as the best in this book.

Classroom Nightmare

It's a dark, depressing gloom
Fog is swirling around the room
Windows rattling
Children chattering
A door creaks open and the air goes still

Molten, fiery eyes light up the dark
A glint of light on teeth razor-sharp
A stench so foul
Then an ear-splitting howl
'You boys and girls, listen well!'

The monster's mouth, a sickening grin
Then a tiny voice squeaking, 'Come in, come in.'
In an instant the monster disappears
I awake from my daydream, just before tears
It's my teacher and she's not that bad
Hooray!

Olivia Bushell (8)
Byfield School, Byfield

My Dream Of The Dream Collector

(Inspired by 'The Sound Collector' by Roger McGough)

A stranger called this morning dressed all in black and grey
Put every dream into a bag and carried them away

The dance of the Fairyland fairies
While I am picking berries
The barking of the dog
The leaping of the frog

The dreamers dancing on the stage
I am flicking through the page
The beeping of the horn
While I am eating corn

The dreams in my bag
Are all very mad
But still they make me happy.

Libby Betts (9)
Bozeat Primary School, Bozeat

The Candy Land Monster

Once there was a Candy Land monster
With no one in Candy Land to play
He wanted to find his big, best mate
He begged and begged each day!

Once he found his friend
He played and played forever
Until his beloved day, for him to always remember

He loved and loved his friend
To eat all their sweets and to play
But later that day they found
Them both on their knees and to say,

'I love you.'

Elize Aimee Lane (10)
Bozeat Primary School, Bozeat

A Walk In The Woods...

There are really colourful leaves
A beautiful badger sett is there
On the edge of all the reeds

I am in the woods
By Everdon's treasure
Wearing my very new hood

I am with my sister
Dad and of course Mum
Caring for me in the sun

I am enjoying walking around
And round and round to the ground
Not having to even pay one pound

Suddenly, I am alone.

Jemima Rose Denny (8)
Bozeat Primary School, Bozeat

Winter Wonderland...

The snow is white
The decorations are bright
I am so looking forward to tonight

It is Christmas Eve
I really want to learn to weave
To make the decorations succeed

Soon Santa will have to leave
For he has children to please

I go to bed
I close my eyes
And wake up to morning shine

But to our dismay Santa has not been
Here to day.

Freyja Clapton (9)
Bozeat Primary School, Bozeat

Monster Of The Forest

Once I was flying on my unicorn and I got very lost,
Obviously I was with my unicorn flying through the sky
'Let us get off!' I cried.

My unicorn was not listening
'Ahh!' I cried. 'We are going to crash!'
We crashed into a tree and landed in a forest.

A giant monster came a few seconds later;
He took me and my unicorn then put us into a deep, dark cave.

Isabel Maeve Pellant (9)
Bozeat Primary School, Bozeat

The Wonderland Dream

Once I dreamed about a wonderland
But then I heard a loud bang
Then I went straight back to my wonderland
A dream came true, I was in it
It was filled with trees but a bug bit me

I wandered around until
I found a fairy land

I walked and walked but they threw stuff at me
I was glad it was just a dream
I never want to go back to
That terrible dream.

Jazmine Farman (10)
Bozeat Primary School, Bozeat

Candy Land And The Candyfloss Fairy!

I woke up in the yummiest of places of all
I searched and searched for a place to stay
Until I found the... candyfloss fairy

When she saw me she fluttered away with a sprinkle here and a sprinkle there
She disappeared in the fluffy sky
I looked around with the gummy bears
We ate through the cupcake mountains
Later we found the candyfloss fairy's castle.

Sapphire Alison Goodes (10)
Bozeat Primary School, Bozeat

My Dreamy Dreams

(Inspired by 'The Sound Collector' by Roger McGough)

A stranger called this morning
Dressed all in black and grey
Put every dream into a bag
And carried it away

The prancing of the kitten
The dancing of the dog
The spells of the princesses
The croaking of the frog

The purring of the cat
The jiggling of the mouse
The shouting of the teacher
The creaking of the house.

Anya Hillyard (9)
Bozeat Primary School, Bozeat

Indian Rag Pickers

R ag pickers deserve a break
A lways working, no sweat all day
G etting wet in the rain every decade

P icking trash all day long
I told the king
'C atch a pile of bling and
K ings.'
E erie eyes stared upon me
'R ight,' he said and
S hot them all dead.

Finley Repton (9)
Bozeat Primary School, Bozeat

I Am Now A Footballer

Once upon a dream
I was a footballer
But I wanted to be a publisher

I was on a green field
I was the goalie
I needed a shield
And shouted, 'Come help me.'

Myles came to block the ball
But the ball hit him
It felt like a rock
The ball went in the bin.

Liam Ross (9)
Bozeat Primary School, Bozeat

It's Snowing

It was warm yesterday
The same with Sunday
I went to bed to realise
When I closed my eyes
From summer to winter
It really gets bitter

When I woke up
I drank from my cup
Only to notice that it was all in my head
When I went to bed.

Caitlyn Margan (7)
Bozeat Primary School, Bozeat

Joy

Throwing the balls
Back onto the pitch
Kicking the balls past the goalie
Defending my team with my friends
Passing to each other
Shooting past the other team
Taking my favourite shiny trophy
As we win.

Myles Jones (10)
Bozeat Primary School, Bozeat

The Beach

I'm at the beach relaxed, excited and calm
I feel the sand tickling my feet
As the waves escape the deep water
I jump in the sea
Where all the fish live
And all the dreams float
As I keep on swimming, collecting dreams
The starfish call me from across the coast to come and play
The wave, the wave, the big, blue wave
Collects me along and along
Put me in the cave of darkness, fear and tragedy
Now my dream is getting darker
I see a shadow so evil and monstrous
What could it be?

Hannah Layard (10)
Brackley CE Junior School, Brackley

A Midnight Walk

I walk alone, the empty road
Not imagining who I'll meet
The night is dark and a chill wind blows
I've walked for hours, my poor feet

Steep, steep, this hill's steep
The peak seems so far away
Sleep, sleep, I fall asleep
I drift towards another day

'Wake up, wake up,' a voice screams
'You're late, you're late,' they scream again
The sun, the sun, is blinding me
I'm glad this dream has gone away.

Samuel Mitchell (11)
Brackley CE Junior School, Brackley

The Nightmare Exam

When I've hit my pillow, I've never sweet dreamed
Only nightmares, horrible tricks of the mind
This time I was in an exam it seemed
and this test wasn't kind
As I wipe the glassy beads of sweat away from my face
The continuous clock ticking churns my stomach over and over
I can't fill in the answers in the blank space!
But then a continuous beating resonates in my ears
I wake up, my face wet with tears
It was only a dream, the nightmare exam is over.

Emily Lawton
Brackley CE Junior School, Brackley

The Dream

Please, please be a dream
Not a nightmare
I'm scared already
Then a vision appeared
A dragon

The dragon was moaning
Moaning about a rock
The rock was cracked
As cracked as can be
After I realised he
Wasn't moaning about the rock

He was moaning about
His egg, it was the moment
Of sadness for me but I
Knew it was all a dream.

Zsuzsanna Mathe (10)
Brackley CE Junior School, Brackley

Midnight Fall

Far away in your dreams, fairies appear
Dancing around golden mushrooms
What are these? I wonder, winged humans?
No, they're too small
Then, the soft breeze stops, the air fills with a horrible stench
The moon gazes at me and I gaze back
New creatures appear but red and angry, they start to bite me
I wake up scared and confused...

Emma Charlotte Rose Williams (10)
Brackley CE Junior School, Brackley

Dreams And Nightmares

D reaming whilst laying here in my bed
R apid eye movement and thoughts in my head
E agerly waiting for the next day to come
A lthough my current dream is far from done
M essing around with my wings, now I can fly
S oon this will be over but it was amazing, I cannot lie

N ightmares, nightmares, they give you a fright
I n this everything disappears out of sight
G randfather clocks falling on top of you
H owever, you get scared, it's hard to get through
T ick-tock, tick-tock, you're running out of time
M onsters and aliens with their gooey slime!
A lthough everything you see is just in your brain
R arely do you manage to outrun the train
E ventually you wake and realise it's not real
S ighing with relief, 'Wow, what an ordeal!'

Daniel James Clayton (10)
Byfield School, Byfield

The Fairy Tea Party

At the bottom of my garden
There is a pretty fairy house
It looks very small
Not even room for a mouse

I shout to my dog Tilly
'Let's have a look over there.'
But she just wags her tail
As if she doesn't care

I move a little closer
And this is what I see
My tooth fairy Florence
And a big pixie

I feel a sense of excitement
Can this really be?
A fluttering little fairy asked,
'Would you like some tea?'

But then I'm awake
And I'm tucked up in my bed
Was this all just a dream
All these fairies in my head?

My dog is acting strange
And has glitter on her face
I feel so happy
She's dancing with such grace

So down the bottom of my garden
I think you'll all agree
Is a pretty cool place
To sit and have tea!

Rosie Turner (8)
Byfield School, Byfield

Superhero

A little girl in the forest was following a track
When a star in the sky shouted, 'I'm back!'
An alien, purple and red, appeared with a burst
And then he said, 'What to do first.'
The little girl was shocked and said, 'OMG!'
As the alien pushed a lady into a tree!
The little girl shouted, 'Hey, pick on someone your own size!'
The naughty alien tripped over in shock and cries
With a whoosh and a bang and a count to zero
The little girl turned into a superhero
She walked to the alien and wiped the tears from his eyes
And sent him flying back into the sky
This is impossible, how could this be?
I look in the mirror and the girl was me.

Chloe Henderson (6)
Byfield School, Byfield

Racing Through The Night

Alone in my boat
With only my golden pup for company
I set off across the sea.
The day is sunny
The sea is calm
All is well, relaxed and free.

Soon the race is on
I lose the other boats
Am I ahead or behind?

The sun goes down
The sky turns dark
I'm cold, frightened and trapped
Blackness all around.

I steer ahead to a warm glow
A lighthouse guides me
I find a harbour
A cluster of boats
I'm safe.

At dawn the warm, friendly sun rises
The terrors of the night are gone
The end of the race
Happiness, my dog, my boat and me.

Alistair Andrew Smith (8)
Byfield School, Byfield

The World Afar

In the distance I could see
A dragon looking back at me
He was not really in disguise
He had eight legs, eight horns, eight eyes!

I was on the cliff, the rocky land
The waves were crashing on the sand
Thunder and lightning in the sky
Then the dragon flew up high

A vortex appeared near a star
It led me to a world afar
I saw nice dragons, and I could not miss
My friends playing tennis!

I was happy because my buddies were there
Then the dragon took me elsewhere
He took me back towards the light
To the rocky cliff, where the sun shone bright.

Sebastian Adkins (8)
Byfield School, Byfield

Lemmy The Dinosaur Slayer

We woke with a start, Lemmy and I
Something stirred in the corner of my eye
As I looked closer I could see
A T-rex prowling around me

Lemmy barked and started to growl
The T-rex got frightened and started to howl
When the T-rex showed his jaws
Lemmy leapt up and used his claws

As the T-rex turned with his fearsome teeth
Lemmy attacked but came to grief
It was so horrible I started to weep
I felt like I was going to sleep
I woke from this nightmare with a feeling of dread
Then turned to see Lemmy asleep in his bed.

Kyran Warne (9)
Byfield School, Byfield

The Day Elise Became A World Gymnast

I stood and waited with my coach
For my turn to approach
I looked all around in the light
And I shivered with fright
It was my turn next on vault
I needed to sprint as fast as Bolt

Then I heard my name and I jumped to the bar
I swung so high, a shooting star
I finally finished bars and pounced to beam
I really felt part of the GB team
Finally my name was called to the floor
A flick and a tuck back, my score began to soar
Then the announcement, 'Elise got gold.'
And my surprise I just couldn't hold.

Elise Danielle Warne (6)
Byfield School, Byfield

Spiders!

Creepy-crawly running fast
Scary, hairy, creeping past
'Yes, it's me, I'm in your dream
'Cause I'm a spider!'

Hiding in a cupboard
Sitting in a crack
First I'm not there
And in a flash I am back!
'Yes, it's me, I'm in your dream
Cause I'm a spider.'

I make you scream
Out loud with fright
Because I might just
Come out tonight
'Because ha ha, I'm in your dream
'Cause I'm a spider!'

Jude O'Connell (9)
Byfield School, Byfield

Bizarre Bakes

First is a cake shaped like an apple
But purple like a plum
Tastes so sweet
And spongy under my thumb

I dreamt I baked a flapjack
Shaped just like a horse
It was brown, gooey and yummy
And I wanted more and more

Then there was rocky road
Just like a dinosaur
And when I bit into it
It let out a big, chocolatey roar

I saw an amazing cake
So chocolatey and smooth
Just like a bubble
And then it moved.

Orla Kate Driscoll (9)
Byfield School, Byfield

Pony Racing

P onies getting lively
O n the race track they go
N eighing to their friends
Y ou're under starter's orders

R ight, let's go
A s we kick on we go faster and faster
C antering closer to the finishing line
I t's close, who is going to win?
N ice pony, we are nearly there
G reat, we have won.

Sophie Shepherd (9)
Byfield School, Byfield

Killer Clown Chase

At midnight the nightmare began
The killer clowns were chopping down trees
With their axes
The moon was shining brightly
In the deep, dark, ghouly forest
The clowns were chasing me all through the forest
With their grinning smiles and their terrifying laughter
At last I tripped on a tree stump
And the clowns pounced on my back
And suddenly I woke up!

Noah Clarke (7)
Byfield School, Byfield

Cupcake Land

Cupcakes are red
The water is sprinkles
And the frosting is my bed
I eat Pringles

Cupcakes are pink
Rainbows are cars
Vimto is my favourite drink
At the top of cupcakes is magical stars

Cupcakes are brown
Flowers are blue
There is the playground
And the animals say, 'Boo!'

Kayleigh Judge (9)
Byfield School, Byfield

Lily The Gymnast

G reat at gymnastics
Y ears of practise
M ount on the beam
N o-handed cartwheel
A nd backhand spring
S traddle tuck and pike jump
T o improve my floor routine
I mprovements to be made to
C atch that gold with my team.

Lily Norman
Byfield School, Byfield

Blossom

B eautiful petals
L ike lovely pink confetti
O ver the whole path
S prinkled on the road
S prinkles on the drive
O ver the green grass
M y gorgeous blossom trees.

Jorja Taylor (7)
Byfield School, Byfield

On The Farm

T yres on the tractor
R ain on the field
A cres and acres
C ars round the farm
T ime for tea
O nion in the ground
R olling in the fields.

Jayden Haynes (6)
Byfield School, Byfield

Unicorn Land

Unicorns are pretty and my favourite pet is a kitty
Unicorns are cute and their horns are magical
Unicorns leap very high
Unicorns are loved a lot
Unicorns are cuddly.

Madison Judge (6)
Byfield School, Byfield

A Dream For Mummy

A spoon full of coffee
A spoon full of sugar
Pour in the water
Stir, stir, stir
That's how I make Mummy's
Perfect cup of coffee.

Sophie Bushell (7)
Byfield School, Byfield

Untitled

I like riding
It is fun
Jumping jumps
Walk, trot, galloping
Brushing my pony
Feeding sugar lumps to him.

Guy Shepherd (6)
Byfield School, Byfield

It All Makes Sense... Not!

I once dreamt
I was standing astride a ship
The captain was Simon Cowell
He had five heads and twenty-two eyes
And his butt was covered by a sock!

'Argh!' he shouted
'Let's rob the bank
Of its plastic plants!'
'Why don't we steal the money?'
Shouted his best friend, Hoist Themainsail

'That's a no from me,'
Cried the captain, in a Welsh accent
'Let us take the plants!'
Now I was freaked out
I was also flabbergasted, at his petrifying shape!

We were soaring through the air
Surrounded by floating jellyfish
Eating smiling eggs
Their round shapes floating through the void
Laughing in the jellyfish mouths

'That's another no from me,' said the terrifying captain
My pet pebble, Kevin, quivered on my shoulder

Suddenly, Themainsail toppled off the ship
'Worst fall ever - that's three nos from me
Kindly leave the stage!' cried the captain
I woke up, shuddering
It was all a dream.

Matthew Lewis (10)
Fulbourn Primary School, Fulbourn

The Dream Mixture

My dreams can be full of bliss
Sometimes sealed with the perfect kiss
My dreams can be full of fear
Sometimes not being able to hear

I must run away from monster men
Instead of hiding in my den
I could fall and fall and fall
And never be able to speak or call

I could fall in love again
And be the best of all the men
I could win the hardest game
To give my team a vital gain

My family would die alone
And the last thing I did was groan and moan
Sometimes I cannot run
Then I get told my life is done...

I get to play with all my friends
And run and laugh around the bends
I'd be the greatest hero
Instead of being another zero

Now you see my imagination
And my mind is filled with the greatest creation
No one can see what I see
And I will be the best me...

Samuel George (11)
Fulbourn Primary School, Fulbourn

Rabbit Land

I was walking in this mysterious place
Wondering what I would see
I saw something jumping in the distance
What could it be?

As I wandered around and explored
I went through a golden gate
There I found a sign saying:
'Everyone is invited, don't be late!
Come to the royalty rabbit palace
At twenty past three
There we'll have a scrumptious tea!'

Then I saw an arrow
And I knew where I had to go
Some rabbits came leaping past
And I couldn't keep screaming, 'Whoa!'

I followed them to the golden palace
To eat chocolate cake
I didn't even want
To think of being late

But then I found myself
Waking up already

To find myself trying to
Eat up my teddy!

Rosa Grimley Evans (10)
Fulbourn Primary School, Fulbourn

My Dream

As I went to my bed about to sleep
There was a wonderland waiting for me
A small wooden wardrobe stood there looking like it was calling my name
I walked closer and spotted a cupcake on the table
Mmm delicious, it looked really tasty so I ate it
Something didn't feel right
I realised that I was shrinking
And then I started thinking
Maybe now that I'm small I can go through this little wardrobe
Nervously I walked through
I saw a unicorn
It led me to a palace made of gold and crystals and a sculpture of a cupcake
I quickly ran in and realised everyone looked upset
I asked why and a man said,
'The queen's been kidnapped.'
I was about to reply
When everywhere turned pitch-black
And I woke up...

Dilara Cifci (9)
Fulbourn Primary School, Fulbourn

My Dreams Are Like...

My dreams are like leopard geckos clambering up wet leaves
Their stunning patterns shine
My dreams are like poison dart frogs leaping rapidly from leaf to leaf
Warning off predators with their dazzling colours
My dreams are like tropical birds flocking on to the canopy in countless numbers
Their vibrant colours blinding me
My dreams are like ants in mid parade
Their long procession as vast as a tree is tall
My dreams are like tropical storms, pattering down on the canopy above
A swirling mass in the sky
My dreams are like a clear blue sky
Dominating the atmosphere, as vast as the sea
My dreams are like raindrops washing my worries away
Never to be seen again.

Erin Burling (11)
Fulbourn Primary School, Fulbourn

Prison Life!

Leaning down for the beautiful necklace
With Iggy by my side
Doing her laces
While on the phone

A police car arrived by the side of me
Saying they have to arrest me
'Why?' I asked
'You have completed your task...
Robbing Iggy's home!'

They pushed me into the car
With handcuffs on my hands
I cried

When we arrived
My mum standing there surprised
She said she was disappointed
And to this day I'm still haunted...
By her

Living in this cell
In my head is a bell
Mum's voice going through my head
I thought Iggy was my friend
Destroyed I let out my tears

My life has become quite dull
My heart is empty.

Libby Jarvis (10)
Fulbourn Primary School, Fulbourn

The Disastrous Dream

I am a king
I wear a suit of a superhero
My hands can magically create anything - money
Machines, monsters
My house is made of trampolines and cake
I swim in my massive pool
I love my spa
But one day something bad happened
I went outside to play when I saw something -
It was a clown, a scary clown
I ran inside and locked all the doors
I looked out the window and saw a monster
It picked up my house and threw it
My palace smashed
And the clowns walked in
I made a gun with my hands and shot the clowns
One of the clowns came behind me and punched me
My eyes shot open in my bed.

Charlie Rickett (10)
Fulbourn Primary School, Fulbourn

Dreams

Bright lights twinkling like stars
Bright lights flashing
Bright lights flashing
Bright lights as bright as the sun
A crowd as crazy as noisy monkeys
The crowd is jumping with joy
A drummer is drumming the drums
A guitarist strumming the guitar
A pianist playing the piano
I'm in a band
I'm in London
I'm on a stage
I feel famous
I'm rich
I'm the leader of the band
We live at a cool rock star house
With a guitar-shaped chimney
And a door shaped as a drum
The house is striking purple and black in colour
Bright lights flashing
Bright light flashing.

Hanna Stewart
Fulbourn Primary School, Fulbourn

People Trying To Get Away

P eople trying to get away
O pening their door to fire machine guns
L ooking at all the glass smash
I shoot back
C overing our heads from the bullets
E ach bullet passes my head

C hasing them still
H aving one of their tyres popped
A s they nearly crash
S hooting the other tyres
E ach bullet we fired hit the air

D riving into a wall
R unning to the car
E ach of their guns, broken
A t the car the keys were broken and snapped
M any things broke.

Logan Neilson (10)
Fulbourn Primary School, Fulbourn

My Dreams Are Like...

My dreams are like cockatoos chirping softly
My dreams are like giant land snails slithering across my hand
My dreams are like leopard geckos darting around
My dreams are like a bearded dragon threatening its predator
My dreams are like hamsters squeaking in love
My dreams are like puppies crowding around me
My dreams are like cats sleeping on my lap
My dreams are like snakes slithering across me
My dreams are like the sunshine beaming on us
My dreams are like the rain dripping on the rooftops
My dreams are like rainbows with gold at the end.

Mischa Shipton (10)
Fulbourn Primary School, Fulbourn

My Dreams

My dreams are like penguins, soaring in the Antarctic seas
My dreams are like badgers, rustling through the multicoloured leaves
My dreams are like squid, diving into my mind
My dreams are like octopuses, squeezing into all of the hidden corners of my brain
My dreams are like snails, slowly munching the green grass
My dreams are like raindrops, dripping on my face
My dreams are like snowflakes, melting on my nose
My dreams are like sunshine shining, sparkling on the planet Earth.

Victoria Vireikyte (10)
Fulbourn Primary School, Fulbourn

Nightmare Horse

Here I am
Again to die
In nowhere
Will he come or will he not?
The cold air pierces my skin
I stand waiting
My hair flailing
My teeth chattering
I stand alone, emotionless
Trying to feel love
I feel none
My heart is grey
Then it happened
He appeared
The horse of nightmares
He rears
I run
I've learnt one thing though
Never turn around.

Alex Matthew Marson (10)
Fulbourn Primary School, Fulbourn

A Dream Is An Infinite Paradox

A dream is a paradox
Which you are able to be free
An eternal reality
Which your mind pretends to be

A dream is like a marshmallow
Or maybe some dough
You can go where you want
And make it your own!

A dream can also be dark, however
Become a nightmare
Make you want to wake up
Like being chased by a bear.

Sam Gurney
Fulbourn Primary School, Fulbourn

Dreams

Here I am standing with a gulp
I move my mouse to my subscription box
And say, 'OMG.'
100 million subs
Am I dreaming?
Let me get a wet flannel
Please say I'm a wake
Yes!
Let me make a celebration video
Two minutes later, ding
From YouTube
'You have got the
Emerald play button!'

Bjorn Ford (10)
Fulbourn Primary School, Fulbourn

My Dreams Are Like...

My dreams are like gazelles jumping with happiness all over
My dreams are like pugs, as soft as a pillow and warm
My dreams are like cheetahs, hunting for prey
My dreams are like snow dropping on my face
My dreams are like lightning, lighting up my brain
My dreams are like thunderclouds, clogging up my brain.

Su-Ad Tungteiya Musah (10)
Fulbourn Primary School, Fulbourn

My Perfect Dream

My perfect dream would be dancing in the Strictly Come Dancing final
My perfect dream would be dancing with Aljaz
My perfect dream would be standing there waiting for the results
My perfect dream would be walking off the dance floor with the glitter ball trophy
My perfect dream would be me, a dancing hero.

Eva Patey (10)
Fulbourn Primary School, Fulbourn

My Dreams Are Like...

My dreams are like kittens purring softly
My dreams are like jaguars prowling the land
My dreams are like fish swimming in my mind
My dreams are like the sunshine scorching my mind
My dreams are like rainfall cooling my mind
My dreams are like fluffy snow on a freezing
winter day.

Bailey James (10)
Fulbourn Primary School, Fulbourn

My Dream

I dream of a lovely magic world full of happiness
Where your wishes start where you want
Where poor people become rich
And when they are helping the people and others

I dream of a world full with people
Where they can't be jealous
And give each other money.

Charlie Austwick (10)
Fulbourn Primary School, Fulbourn

A Dream...

A dream is just like paradise, only in your mind
You do not know what will happen or what you'll find
It's a place you cannot ignore
When you close your eyes it's just next door
While you are sleeping there is no weeping
You won't be upset anymore.

Lisa Distill (11)
Fulbourn Primary School, Fulbourn

Shadow Friends!

Shadow, shadow, how are you?
Hi shadow, it's great to see you
At that precise moment
Shadow you did different things
Didn't you?
Own up!
You just want to be my friend

When I dance, you sing
When I hide, you seek
When I eat you drink
When I say never you say forever
I love you shadow

Shadow, shadow, I love you
Hey shadow, we're friends too
Very good friends
Even if you weren't my shadow
I would still love you.

Holly Carol Rowland (10)
Great Creaton Primary School, Creaton

London Bridge Is Down

Watching the wave immensely crash over the tatty London Bridge,
really sent a tingle throughout my body.
The London Bridge clattered down.
All of the bricks tumbled down.
Everyone was in deep danger.
Struggling,
Screaming,
Shouting.
People hurried, trying to get out, whilst fading
Into the shiny, roaring river.
Immediately, I called the police.
Impatiently, I stood waiting for the police to put
a barrier around.
For no one to go on.
It was so intense, my heart made it to the back of my throat.
My body swollen with fear.
My heart filled with screams and people crying for help.
The police entered the river with boats.
Searching for all of the people.
Ten minutes later they found all of the people
And took them to land.

I awoke, it was all a dream.
Or was it?

Isla Draper (10)
Kingsfield Primary School, Chatteris

The Star Night

The colourful balloons galloped into the sky
Like a horse running from a snake
Swaying over everything

The glistening moon
Roaring at me
My legs were waving in fear
I was right to be scared

The elegant stars posing
While I kept bumping into them
Furiously they stared at me
Determined
Struggling
Gripping
Clinging

Lights, shouting
No longer able to see me, no longer able to see help
I trembled with fear
Slipping out of my hand
Falling down to Earth

I gripped tight to the string
Is this the end?
I thought as I let go of the string

Halfway out of Earth
Suddenly I woke
Was it a dream?

Phoebe Kate Moore (10)
Kingsfield Primary School, Chatteris

Scary Day Or Dream

The cliff is crumbling dangerously
Seeing it fall is like rain atrociously cascading from a bad day

A road, grey and unforgiving
Cars driving, it's a whirlwind
As I cross the road I'm full of fear

My bike looks snazzy but it's dangerous
Nuts and bolts are a major hazard
As I whoosh through the air, I wish I was safe

The river is swaying past my face
Feeling a bright splash of air going past me
It was my fear mocking me in my path

Frightened, scared
I'm so petrified it was as if my doom was disintegrating beneath my feet
Suddenly I woke up! It was a dream, or was it?

Jamie Toth (10)
Kingsfield Primary School, Chatteris

The Night At The Haunted House

The ancient lights glowed dimly through the
senior window
Stalking me
Like a creepy person

The cursed trees creaking
Trembling with terror
They were right to be frightened

The blood-curdling from the shadows screaming ahead
They knew I longed to be there
But instead I was caught

Strolling
Standing
Screaming

The ghost thrashed
So loud I could no longer hear my heart
Pulsating in my ears
Fiercely roared in my face, I faced forward
Determined

Battling forward
Springing, trudging
Standing in the dark deaths.

Ellie Bissett (10)
Kingsfield Primary School, Chatteris

The Wave

Quietly the wave began to rumble like a volcano about to erupt
As it got bigger, I got braver
When it reached its full potential, I had the courage to fight like a true hero in battle
The deadly wave spat as I progressed along its curling, lumpy tongue of doom
I was getting faster but so was the wave
As I looked back, I saw the wave
Thrashing behind fiercely
It was getting louder and I was getting smaller
But somehow further away
When there was no wave left, I felt like the winner
As I got to shore.

Ryan Fell (10)
Kingsfield Primary School, Chatteris

The Cold, Frosty Morning

The cold frost suffocated the emerald grass
As the clouds sedately slumbered in the light blue sky
The secretive goal spied on the frosty blanket

The timber trees slowly pranced in the wind
While the tired ground dozed under the freezing frost
The boiling sun ducked behind the chocolate
bony trees
Opening one gleaming eye

The light back shadows crept in the arctic frost
Stretching their giant bodies
The cyan sky watched over the Earth
As the lazy goal slept in the ground.

Rosey Ford (9)
Kingsfield Primary School, Chatteris

That House

As I approached the spooky house I started to tremble in fear
Moving closer I heard footsteps behind me
I turned
Just darkness
Glancing through the front window
A solo light flickered
Furiously, multiple doors slammed in a row
Interrupted by an echoing scream
Then silence
This contrast was terrifying
Anxiously I wandered over to the door
Suddenly the door came flying open
Unsure, I stepped inside
The door slammed closed behind me...

Kendra Mae North (10)
Kingsfield Primary School, Chatteris

An Autumn Day

The sleep walking clouds crawled slowly
Across the beautiful sky
The sun unlocked one worn-out eye
Creeping into the wide day
With the daydreaming earth
As the illuminated light comes into view
Shadows creep from the hills
Slinking across the snowy grass
As the delicate sky drifts softly along the atmosphere
swaying with the wind
Blowing across
The spying football goal peers carefully at the icy ground
Standing on the frosty grass.

Wiktoria Julia Drobisz (11)
Kingsfield Primary School, Chatteris

A Frosty Morning

Yawning, the sun opened one weary eye
Crawling carefully from depths of the Earth
The shadows crept out of hiding
Stopping the light from spreading

The trees were undulating with the wind
Barging through
As the clouds gracefully glided above
The light shone through them

The frost covered the emerald grass
The icy blades danced in the wind
The sky watched over the field
Pale blue in the bright light.

Ellie-Mae Jarvis
Kingsfield Primary School, Chatteris

The Haunted House

I stalked through the forest
The wind swayed the trees
It was eerie

When I stalked through the forest
The sky fading into darkness
I was frightened

The old crows squawked on top
Of something that I couldn't really see
I was petrified

I was at the edge of the forest
I saw a creepy house
I slowly stalked up the stairs
And opened the door... ahhhhh!
I woke up, was it a dream or not...?

Olivia Mae Pacey (10)
Kingsfield Primary School, Chatteris

The BMX

The colourful BMX was like
A rainbow in the sky
As it flew through the air

Gradually the ramp leaned towards the middle
About to catch the colourful bike
And the ramp opened to make the jump difficult

Leaning in the air
Twisting and turning before
The dead lights went off
Terrified

The lights came back on
The biker landed on the ground
The biker was fresh like a bit of solid gold.

Callum Cooper
Kingsfield Primary School, Chatteris

In The Morning

The sun carefully crawled from his mysterious hiding place
The massive fireball pushed his hands through the branches
Unlocking the secrets of the shadows
The misty creatures lay on the raw blanket

The frost suffocated the lush grass
As the fiery star streaked off the crisp ground
The trees danced around the outside of the chilly ballroom
As they stretched for the day ahead.

Evan Harte (10)
Kingsfield Primary School, Chatteris

The Shally House

The house stalks me
Like a scary person following
The haunted, shally house is in front of me
Trembling fear, in the darkness
It is right to be scared
The quiet house scares me
It feels I shouldn't be here
But I had nightmares
The wind whooshes so cold that I can't feel my hands
Four steps forward, entering the dark, scary house full with bats
I woke up, it was just a nightmare.

Jayden Mcdonnell
Kingsfield Primary School, Chatteris

Winter Breeze

Slowly the sun stretched its burning, buttery arms
Creeping from behind the Earth
As the light appeared
Shadows emerged from behind the horizon
The leafy trees stretched their khaki arms
As pearl frost suffocated the fresh, green grass
The ivory clouds still could not be bothered to wake up
The snow-white goal waited listlessly for a match
Finally the world woke up.

Declan O'Neill (10)
Kingsfield Primary School, Chatteris

The Crisp Field

The exhausted trees yawned lethargically
Inaudibly standing guard over the crisp field
The sweltering sun woke up
Leisurely edging from its hiding place under the deep ground
The fluffy clouds danced smoothly
While ambling towards the dazzling sun
The suffocating frost hugged the ground
Cold and wet, while left shivering
Finally the world woke up.

Kieran Fisher (10)
Kingsfield Primary School, Chatteris

The Bright Day

The bright, creamy sun reluctantly opened one eyelid
As I rose past the bony trees
The freezing frost tried to grip and hold on
But the vigour of the lights sun sucked it up
The bony trees smoothly swung in the misty wind
As the blue sky clouds drove past in
The aquamarine sky softly breathed
As quietly as a whisper
Brushing the tiny, thin twigs.

Jake Singleton (11)
Kingsfield Primary School, Chatteris

The Sunny Morning

The dark shadows crept through the light of the sun
Suddenly prowling through the icy frost
The scorching sun awoke to greet the world
As sunrise had just begun
The muddy ground rested underneath the frost
Icy and cold
The beige tree waved to the sun
As the shadows came out to play
The lonely goal waited patiently for the next football game to begin.

Kai Jack Wiltshire (10)
Kingsfield Primary School, Chatteris

The Wintry Morning

The robust goal peered around the trees as they wreathed it
The timber trees stretched in the morning sky yawning wearily
As day broke the sun crawled up over Earth to wake everyone up
The pearl clouds dancing in the bright, blue sky
As the frost stood in the gleaming golden sun
The soaring shadows stared along the field
Waiting for somebody to come.

Logan Barbault (10)
Kingsfield Primary School, Chatteris

A Forest Poem

The drowsy trees yawned reluctantly
As they slowly elongated their bony branches
The blistering sun opened one gleaming eye
As it crawled up from the horizon

The ivory clouds sleepwalked cautiously
As they stalked across the never-ending sky
The light black shadows emerged from the towering trees
And prowled along the forest floor.

Tegan Smith (11)
Kingsfield Primary School, Chatteris

The Icy Morning

The listless trees yawned sluggishly
Stretching their bony branches
The sparkly sun opened one drowsy eye
Tiptoeing from its hiding place behind the towering trees
The gloomy shadows slowly emerged
Walking across the raw ground
The freezing frost
Slowly suffocated the grass.

Lois Wills (10)
Kingsfield Primary School, Chatteris

A Poem About Nature

The terrifying trees glared at the sky
Ready to pounce on anything dangerous
The frost strangled the grass
Like a predator
The sun stretched to the top of the sky
Nearly crashing with a blast
The clouds shuffled through the sky
Making shapes of all kinds.

Ewa Maria Slowik (9)
Kingsfield Primary School, Chatteris

The Crisp, Broken Leaves

The white, fluffy clouds were stretching
Their bellies wide and narrow
The sun opened one gleaming eye and yawned
It shone through the trees
Crawling from its bed
The trees wriggled as they woke up
Enjoying the warmth of the sun.

Callum Fitzpatrick (10)
Kingsfield Primary School, Chatteris

BMX Race

Worriedly the metal BMX waits
Feeling worried the BMX might have a flat tyre
The bike is orange and yellow like fire
The ramp is still
I'm just staring at the silver ramp
The tall, black and brown mounting behind the ramp.

Lewie Bond (10)
Kingsfield Primary School, Chatteris

Poem About Nature

The golden clouds crept quietly
across the restless blue sky
The hills were frozen like the ground is always freezing
The restless clouds watched down over everyone going
for a walk.

Harry Henman
Kingsfield Primary School, Chatteris

Frozen Morning

The tired clouds sleepily danced across the sky as they gazed at the Earth
While the sun woke up, it shone through the trees
The frost was standing guard
Suffocating the grass.

Layla Casey Hobson (10)
Kingsfield Primary School, Chatteris

GTA5 Ramp

Swiftly, the cold river flowed through the roofs
The boy coolly jumped off the rusty ramp
The mountains were as big as a hot-air balloon
The bike creaked over the old, wooden ramp.

Jamie Harrington (10)
Kingsfield Primary School, Chatteris

A Mythical Land

I slowly drifted into a dream
But it wasn't a dream that made me scream
Somehow I was in such a rush
I had to turn and call the bus
No bus was there so I called for Alicorn
Away, away, away I flew
Up into the sky so blue
I went to see white, big Yeti
But he wasn't there, such a pity
Away I soared to see King Phoenix
Then he said...
'How old are you; five or six?'
I think my jumper was a bit too much
Then appeared two servants of his
They seemed to be in such a tizz
Loch Ness monster and gnome bright green
Quietly said...
'You won't believe what we've just seen!
The fairies have come out of their hollow tree!
Princess Starburst and Prince Blancmange
Have come to meet her majesty the queen.'
I ran towards the palace gates
And there I saw my old dream mates

The carriage screeched as it came to a halt
But sadly I must leave my dream to have breakfast
To be like Usain Bolt!

Elizabeth Wain (9)
Paulerspury CE Primary School, Paulerspury

Once Upon A Dream

I sit down on my cosy, warm YouTube chair,
The views hit me like a tank surrounding me
And bouncing around like a rubber ball,
It feels like an honour to be cheered on by my fans
Everyone feels excited to see me
Burning all the dislikes, keeping all the likes
Comments keep me happy like:
'Awesome!'
'Fabulous!'
'Great!'
'My hero!'
'Keep up the good work!'
Feeling out of breath
The videos go *bang, pow, pow*
Throwing away the haters and keeping the likers
Everyone should subscribe to me
Jumping from a diving board into a pool of subscribers
All my fans say 'Hip hip hooray!'

Kieran Ames (11)
Scartho Junior School, Grimsby

Life Of A Policewoman

As I jump into
My chariot the tyres
Whisk me to danger.

Sirens are wailing
Voices shouting, heart pounding
Nerves taking over.

At last I arrive,
At the crime scene I can see:
Blood puddles, bodies.

Wanted criminals,
One down, one to be found,
Click, click, arrested.

As I return,
I hear loads of thank yous because
The streets are safer.

Keira Tupman (11)
Scartho Junior School, Grimsby

Everest

Slowly trudging through the desolate land,
My thoughts racing
Scattering images; the task looming ahead
Whirling round the forefront of my fevered imagination
A wild feverish.

Jagged rocks cascading from the perilous sky
My pulse thumping
Quickly dodging; my life at stake
Scenarios orbiting round my perplexed mind
A notorious task.

Infinite snow biting at my venerable legs
My head pivoting
Gradually moving; trying to stay active
Situations sprinting round my weary head
An impossible assignment.

Jack Brighton (11)
Scartho Junior School, Grimsby

Tuna

Catching a tuna is like catching a whale,
Compared to that beast I am like a snail
The fish feel like a car in the mysterious waters
Their eyes are screaming, 'I am surprised
You caught us.'
As I give them to the restaurant
They make a big fuss
Now I go off to catch some more
And after I have, I evacuate to shore
I relax on the smooth sand
And after I sell my fish, I will make few grand.
As usual I sail out to sea
Catching tuna is as hard as catching a bee!

Ben Connolly (10)
Scartho Junior School, Grimsby

Royalty

To be on a throne
To wear a crown
To rule the land
And not see a frown

The air as fresh as mints
The palace as spacious as the sea
The people working together
And the land full of glee

So problems run away
So the people are full of joy
So there's not a concern to be seen
And the children clash with their toys

What else can I do?
What needs need fulfilling?
What else shall I conclude?
And the people are chilling.

Annas Mohamed (11)
Scartho Junior School, Grimsby

Snow Dreaming

S now is everywhere I glance
N ow the race has started
O n the way to the finish, I
W atch the scenery of the Himalayas
B usy machines work all day
O h, I am nearly there
A final flying squirrel
R iding down I spot the finish and...
D one - my race is over
I came first, the crowd cheering
N o longer in adrenaline
G oing home, ready for some hot chocolate.

Oliver Wiseman (10)
Scartho Junior School, Grimsby

Once Upon A Dream

Bouncing
Jumping
Flipping around,
Rolling
Laughing
Above the ground.

Dreaming
Hoping
Wanting more,
Bigger
Funner
Never a bore.

Running
Tumbling
Into a foam pit,
Crawling
Diving
Fun, I admit.

Smiling
Laughing
Compact with glee,

Leaving
Believing
The trampoline will be mine!

Lawrence Jackson (11)
Scartho Junior School, Grimsby

Strictly Come Dancing

S wiftly, I floated across the floor,
T en was coming my way.
R ocking from side to side,
I glided away.
C lapping engulfed my ears.
T owering above heads, the orb of sparkle shone,
L ighting up the steps,
Y et soon it would be gone.

I had won!

Elizabeth Holliday (10)
Scartho Junior School, Grimsby

Parkour Dreams

Pouncing over obstacles.
A backflip, a front flip - still going.
Running, jumping, flipping over the walls that are in my way.
Obstacles block my path so I gash over them.
Under, over - few obstacles left.
Racing to the end but one obstacle stands in my way to win
It's over! Victory is mine.

Finlee Robinson (11)
Scartho Junior School, Grimsby

Once Upon A Dream

Take your marks... *Beep!*
Holding my breath, diving deep
Straight as a pencil
Starting my swim
Gliding to victory
First length is done
Turning around
A fresh start
Speeding along
In first place now!
Five metres away from victory
Touching the wall
First place is mine!

Ben Rendall (11)
Scartho Junior School, Grimsby

A Fizzy Fantasy Bouncing World

Pink, fluffy marshmallows, laying in their river of cries
The shady moon covered in cheesy cheese
Everything spicy but sweet
Mermaids throwing pillows and tantrums
Candyfloss turning around
Snowflakes raising glasses saying, 'Hey!'
Liking arms and staring deeply
Nobody sees the moon shouting
A random hand pokes me in my dream
I suddenly hear familiar sounds
Seems like it was all a dream
Disappointed I seem
But why?
If it was all a dream
I feel emotionally ignored and irritated
I started to build up fear for no absolute reason
Silly me why did I build up excitement
I wondered if it was actually a dream?
Weirdly for me it feels like everything's possible...
But a dream...

Elizabeth Boamah (10)
The Arbours Academy, Northampton

Creepy Clown

I was sitting down, I saw a very creepy clown
As soon as I decided to run he decided to pull out a gun
I had to stop
Then I heard a pop
This time I heard a bell
Suddenly I fell
What could I do?
Hope that he did not take my baby too
Surely he could not be too much harm
But then I saw blood on his palm
Then I realised I had to stop
I just had to give up
It was just too much
Then it came to me
This can't be real
It's all fake
It must be a mistake.

Denroy Welsh (10)
The Arbours Academy, Northampton

Dance, Sing, Sleep

Have you ever sang with mermaids?
Slept with unicorns
Or danced with fairies?
Well I have in my dream
It was a dream that I wish could come true
All I could imagine was that dream
I had to follow it
Daydreams or night dreams
That's all I think about
But one day it got so big I had to do something
My whole life changed
My dream came true
I loved my life
I loved singing with the mermaids
Sleeping with the unicorns
And dancing with the fairies.

Rutendo Mashapa (9)
The Arbours Academy, Northampton

The Old Galaxy

I floated through space like a snail in a case
But all I could make was sepia rusting the world
And a giant Earth filled with birth
But while I glanced at the nearby Earth
A figure with a hat bigger than a mat appeared in the cotton candy cloud
The figure that I saw was a carriage holding the Lincoln reign
Neigh the horses went as they rode past me
The galaxy danced and the planets sang in the distant darkness.

Bartosz Kaczmarczyk (10)
The Arbours Academy, Northampton

Famous Dancer

Come back, come back
To Unicorn Land
My soul is blank, my head is bland
Since you left me it has been so quiet
My heart desires for my famous dancer
Kate, come back, we need your laughter
There is no turning back from your happily ever after
If you leave again take me with you
No more turning back or I will not be with you
Hurry, time is running out, I need you Kate like you need me.

Abbie Elizabeth McCallum (10)
The Arbours Academy, Northampton

My Nightmare

As I sleep, I hear a noise in the hallway
A shadow starts to fade away
I lift my cover over my head
My heart feels like lead
One tear cascades down my face
A multicoloured creature starts to pace
I peek from above my cover
And try to shout to my mother
But silence was only heard
This nightmare was my third
My candle roars and blows out
What was all of this about?

Aliyah White (10)
The Arbours Academy, Northampton

Killer Clown!

K illing is their passion and destiny
I llusion, blood and hammers
L ocked down to kill
L augh until death
E erily stalking in the night
R eally rude and rotten

C ar horns blaring in the distance
L onging for kidneys
O ut for revenge
W e are dripping
N o heart left.

Dylan Jake Carey (10)
The Arbours Academy, Northampton

Is It Magic?

I am so magical
This is so magical
I have the power
The power of the dragon fire
Nothing has prepared me for this power
It is making me powerful
But it's out of control
If I continue to train with my mother
Then I can be a super heroine
When I fly
I fly through the whistling wind
I am so magical
This is so mythical.

Larissa Grimmer (10)
The Arbours Academy, Northampton

Killer Clown

K iller clown hiding
I n blood and tears
L iquorice boots
L ingering energy
E ntering a hall of nightmares and fears
R inging doorbells, time to hide

C lock is ticking
L oud like a lion
O n a journey to the death of life
W hat should I do?
N owhere to run.

Owen Shrubb (10)
The Arbours Academy, Northampton

My Monstrous Nightmare

Running violently, through a wood
Trees alive
Thunder roaring, lighting flashing
Wearily as I take a step forward
Thud!
What was that?
Images of frozen animals etched on my eyelids
Now flowing wild through my mind
Sweat pours like a waterfall cascading down my head
Something is coming for me,
Death is now my best friend...

Reyhana Rahman (10)
The Arbours Academy, Northampton

Shooting Stars In The Night Sky!

The shooting stars dived into the volcano
Constellation
Crashing and dashing under and over, side to side
Stars flipped and skipped
Kaleidoscopic colours burst through the night sky

As the field twinkled in the night sky
We laid as if we were on holiday
The grass was our little blanket as we fell asleep.

Stephine Akingbehin (10)
The Arbours Academy, Northampton

Lovely Horses

I wish, I wish I could have a pet horse
Horses are as fun as swimming in a pool
Clip-clop, clip-clop go the horses
The horses dance while they are listening to music
Every time I see them
I just want to ride them
When I touch them I want them
Every time I look around I imagine them walking around me.

Taya Swartz (9)
The Arbours Academy, Northampton

Neymar, My Hero

N eymar the best dribbler in the universe
E legantly, he scores a hat-trick
Y elling and cheering, his fans cry
M y hero
A s quick as lightning that he blazes across the sky
R eaching for the crowds, it's like he is playing just for me.

Jason Asante (9)
The Arbours Academy, Northampton

Clouds

Soaring through the clouds
Clouds like soft bunnies
Eating clouds that tasted like cotton candy
I arrived at a magical place
Made of candy, peppermint, Haribos
Bright colours popped out everywhere
Not one colour missed out of sight.

Katy Dempsey (10)
The Arbours Academy, Northampton

Untitled

Hard chocolate handle
On a hard toffee door
Ginger and frosting base
That you just can't handle
This is your dream just come and see
What can we find?
What can we dream?

Tudor Catrinescu (10)
The Arbours Academy, Northampton

Adventure Dream

I gently close my sleepy eyes
They blink one time like butterflies
Before I know it I'm asleep
Not one more word, no, not a peep
I'm in a world of candyfloss clouds
A caramel house? They must be proud
Look! Big, pink unicorns
With orange, tall horns!

I wander off into the woods
I want to eat the clouds! I would if I could
But, oh! I don't know the way!
Luckily, here are the unicorns to save the day
We go to their house for dinner
Candy apples were my winner
But sadly, now I wake, it's day
What a great dream I've had in May.

Grace Lola Sargent (10)
Welton CE Academy, Welton

The Lonely Alien

Oh how I wish I could go to Earth
But I'm stuck up here sad and lonely
Nobody here to sit with me
I'm different but I don't want to be

As I sit I watch in sadness
I wish, oh I wish I was one of them
I hate it up here where I'm cold and sad
Why am I up here? Have I been bad?

I see them laughing
Joking around
They're all down there having fun
But I'm up here with no happy sun

As the cold shatters
I start to doze off in the sun beams
The sun shines through
Then I wake up, it was all a dream.

India Gries (9)
Welton CE Academy, Welton

A Stalking Monster Nightmare

I stood still, frozen on the spot
Everywhere I looked there was nothing there
I knew something was watching me but I didn't know what
Until I felt it breathing in my hair

I stared at it, right in its eye
I screamed and screamed but no one heard me
I hoped and hoped that I wasn't going to die
I quickly turned around and began to flee

I began to run with all my power
Lots of trees were all I could see
I must have ran for at least an hour
Then all of a sudden I woke to my cup of tea.

Danny Healey (10)
Welton CE Academy, Welton

Shadow

I slipped through the door: the derelict door
I looked either way but all I saw was a pitch-black
blackness that filled either way
I saw a figure in the dark, it stood out as a shimmering,
shining yellow that illuminated the dark
Then it looked at me and made me start
I ran down the hallway as if I were a cheetah
I looked over my shoulder and noticed there was only
a blackness
The next thing I knew I was on the floor
A mysterious shadow next to me and a lot of gore.

Guy Dawkins (11)
Welton CE Academy, Welton

My Horrible Dream

When I fall asleep, close my eyes
I whizz past the land of French fries!
I land in a room and walk outside
And realise I am in the land of spooks
I am as scared as a mouse getting tracked down
As I take a step back as frightened as can be
I look around, and out of the ground shoots some scorching-hot fire
Suddenly, wolves howl around me about to have some lunch
This is what I dread...
So I lift up my head
And realise I am safely tucked in bed!

Isabella Sophia Dunnett (8)
Welton CE Academy, Welton

Nightmares

The time is coming, coming, coming, closer still
The time of intense horror and ever-piercing screams
The time when soothing lights flicker out
The time when the happy dreams turn pitch-black
The time when drooling monsters haunt you
The time of pure horrifying fright in the dark
The time when darkness rules ruthlessly over the land
The time remains still, as you shout out
The time when the remains of happiness die
These are nightmares.

Thomas Carvell (11)
Welton CE Academy, Welton

When I Fall Asleep

When I fall asleep, I close my eyes,
Pretending I am disguised,
In the distance, I see luminous flowers shine at me,
It is a beautiful sight, I see kites go past me.

I go too far, lost, I am nowhere to be seen,
The darkness drops slowly as it gets later and later,
It seems like once upon a dream, nowhere to be seen,
I hear the owls tweet,
As I slowly open my eyes, I know it's just a dream.

Oliver Dunnett (8)
Welton CE Academy, Welton

It's Coming

It's coming, it's creeping up the stairs
Telling me to to go sleep and listen to my nightmares
Scaring me out of my skin
I hear the voice once more
Creeping to my bedroom door
As the door is opened up
I never see its face!
My heart is beating loud and fast
I fear it's come at last
Never have I been so scared
But now the time has come
I barely let my mind think before I shout, 'Mum!'

Claudia Elizabeth Margaret Cater (10)
Welton CE Academy, Welton

Galaxy Dream

G oing to sleep
A fter the alien jumps I doze off
L anding on Mars I feel dizzy
A s I spin colours of the world change
X ylophones play extraordinary tunes
Y ou turn the sky blue, purple and pink

D ozing off to sleep
R oy the alien turns up
E very day I sit on Mars lonely and sad
A fter Roy came I was happier
M y dream was amazing.

Issabella Holt (10)
Welton CE Academy, Welton

Metal Mayhem

I'm in the scrapyard
Looking for pieces for my machine
Oh wait
I see a figure
I call, 'Hello.'
No reply
I turn around
I hear a noise
The figure stops and stares
He strikes fear into my heart
Suddenly he starts to run by my side
I notice a dog with cuts all over him
I hear gunshots
I don't know what to do
I scream
Only to find it's a dream.

Raife O'neill (8)
Welton CE Academy, Welton

My Football Dream

M ake your way over to him
E veryone taking selfies
S triking and defending, he can do that
U nder people's feet with a Megz
T hierry Henry would want to see that

Ö nto Messi, skills him out
Z latan Ibrahimovic can't even do that
I look at Özil and give him a smile
L ooking over other players.

Owen Knox (9)
Welton CE Academy, Welton

Clowns

Clouds curtain the blood-red moon
This must be a dream
Low moans fill the air
Over the bridge, a gang of clowns prance over to me
With no one to help, I ready my fists
They cackle menacingly
Now my sight is hazy
My tongue burns like acid
Slam
I hit the jagged floor and wake up at home
My bedside candle dances weakly, before fading away.

Lucy Nicholls (9)
Welton CE Academy, Welton

My Unicorn Friend

My unicorn friend
Your bright colours make me happy
I bounced over the marshmallow clouds
Your pink and blue tail makes me smile
I came to this lollipop house
It gave me quite a fright
I heard this big licking sound
I wondered what it was
A unicorn came out
Something I had never seen before
As I woke up I didn't want my dream to end.

Lily Beatrice Theobald (10)
Welton CE Academy, Welton

Fairy's Dream

Huge flowers spread like a waterproof dome
Beautiful flowers are the colour of honeycomb
Fabulous fairies fly like shooting stars
Magical and marvellous forest is bigger than Mars
Sky is blue, all is light
Rainbow is exquisitely bright
As the rainbow fades it becomes night
I lay down my sleepy head
As I wake upon my bed.

Evie Elizabeth Winn (10)
Welton CE Academy, Welton

My Worst Dream

I had a sleepover with Lucy one night
We heard a thud!
It was quite a fright
The sky burped, gurgled and spun around
Me and Lucy found
A maze at the end
I grabbed the hand of my scared friend
Shaking like a leaf
We saw the dragon's sharp teeth
As I was about to be eaten in my head
I woke up in my safe bed.

Grace Austin (10)
Welton CE Academy, Welton

Woodland Dream

I am in the beautiful lush fields
Sitting on the lush, green grass
The peaceful singing of the birds
The clear blue sky
The rustling of the birds
The robins singing
The swallows flying
The lake is glistening
The river is twisting and twirling
What's that? I wake up by the noise of my alarm
It was just a dream.

Mimi-Rose Ernest (9)
Welton CE Academy, Welton

Unicorns Are Real!

U nicorns are real
N ot many people believe in them
I think they are really beautiful
C oloured creatures, mine is rainbow
O h what an amazing sight at night
R owing by, seeing a wonderful dance at night
N o one knows, my unicorn is secret.

Mia Grace Ainger-Gamble (9)
Welton CE Academy, Welton

Enchanted Forest

Roses singing like mad
The smell is good, not bad
The luminous blue sky
None of the fairies are wearing a tie
There are beautiful, talking butterflies
Ladybirds don't fly
I can't see any fleas
There are talking trees
It was a really nice dream.

Jessica Souter (9)
Welton CE Academy, Welton

The Other Side Of The Land

At the other side of Dream Land
Is a nightmare of beasts and monsters
It is forbidden by Dream Land as it will destroy them
And is your worst fear and more
So run and run and run and run until you wake up
So step on in if you dare and witness the other side!

Matias Rusailh (8)
Welton CE Academy, Welton

A Monster's Dream

I'm in Nightmare Land
Where it is compete darkness
All I have is a fluffy dog
And killer clowns surround me
I am so terrified
Organs drop everywhere
Blood rain falls on the organs and makes them red
Lives fall on the horizon.

Alexander Paul Cater (9)
Welton CE Academy, Welton

Elliot The Dragon

Elliot and me
By the faraway tree
Elliot hides
He uses his disguise
The day is over
I climb the tree
I say, 'Bye'
Then I cry
I lay down my sleepy head
Then I find myself in bed.

Erin Middleton (9)
Welton CE Academy, Welton

Dinosaur Land!

Fast asleep dinosaurs I see
Dinosaurs live quite happily
All around is sunny
The dinosaurs sleep in peace
No one here is nice
Peace and quiet is happy for Dinosaur Land.

Samuel White (10)
Welton CE Academy, Welton

London Dreams

L ondon is my favourite place but I have never seen Queen Elizabeth's castle, but anyway, I am seeing dancers competing. I got tickets for 'Come Along With Me'

O n my unicorn, Fluff is her name, I just love her by the way, she is mine for today

N ow I am going to see the dancers competing, come along, it's time for the show, let's go

D one my job, watching the show, not finished yet, let's watch some more

O h no, the show has finished, let's go home

N ow I am sad, I didn't want to be but I enjoyed the show, but now it's gone

D ancing in the rain, dancing in the sun, made me happy now let's have some fun

R unning to the field and back, swinging on the swing, making me happy, now join in

E ventually, it's time for me to go to bed, it had not ended yet

A cup of cocoa, brush my teeth, brush my hair, it's still not ended yet

M ake some toast, put my PJs on, eat my toast, one last song

S o long, the sun has gone to bed and so must I, goodnight.

Isabelle Dannatt (8)
Wootton St Andrew's Primary School, Wootton

Once Upon A Dream

Once there was a unicorn who could fly so high he could reach the end of the sky
No one could see him, it was pitch-black
Clouds were his home, he slept on them and even made cloud pies
Everything was different to Earth, there was nothing except the planets and space

Until one day a big bang happened in space, there was colour, there was grass, there was everything
People could see the unicorn and they could also see the magical wonders
Occasionally, the unicorn came down to say hello
Nothing was dark, it was spectacular

And the unicorn was ever so happy, he was over the moon!

Darkness was nowhere to be seen
Red roses appeared on Jupiter
Elephants appeared on Saturn
And it was all good
More wonders came every single day.

Isla Grace Turner (9)
Wootton St Andrew's Primary School, Wootton

Beds And Eggs

The bed was doing something
It started to hail
It was funny, it looked like oil
Something came out
It looked like a spout

Then an egg came out
100s and 100s came out at once
Then it stopped
I got on the bed, it started to rock
The bed lifted off the ground

Then went out the window
The eggs shot the birds
I could see the sky
Then I looked at my thigh
It was bleeding because I was in the sky
The bed went faster and faster
Then the eggs were coming out
I almost fell out
I needed to shout

As soon as I knew it
The bed ride was coming to an end
I was going faster than normal

I was going to the future
Then I stopped at the ocean, then everything went slow motion.

Joseph Crowe (9)
Wootton St Andrew's Primary School, Wootton

Dance Darcey

Once, a girl called...

D arcey dreamed of being a famous dancer
A nd meeting Darcey the famous dancer
N ever ever I will be mean to her
C aring means sharing
E ventually, she got poorly so we should be kind, I got a letter saying, 'Meet me, Darcey, at Black and White World'. Then I was amazed, so then I was crazy! So I went off the next day

D arcey is an amazing dancer
A nd I want to be famous too
R ight away I went in the car and drove off
C olours appeared but when I went forward it got dull
E ventually she was better so I went dancing
Y ellow sunshines do not appear in this world, she looked amazing when I saw her.

Darcey Siron (8)
Wootton St Andrew's Primary School, Wootton

Thrown Out!

Once upon a dream
I was a famous wizard
Teaching at a school of witchcraft and wizardry
called Hogwarts
At Hogwarts I teach defence against the dark arts
The most helpful subject of all
Because the darkest wizard called Voldemort
Is going to take over the world

On Monday 17th June
The bell rang for lessons
And the six years came for dark arts

When we started stunning
A boy called Neville Longbottom stunned a girl called
Hermione Granger
And the spell was that strong it stunned her
Until the end of the lesson

The next day I thought I would be thrown out
And guess what?
I was thrown out
And I was never a teacher again.

Jake Nutt (9)
Wootton St Andrew's Primary School, Wootton

In A Galaxy Far Away!

Stars twinkling bright
Like little shiny beads of light
Fireworks
Blues
Purples and greens
That fly and gleam in the air
Like you and me everywhere

The moon is full in the sky
Stars around it means it does not lie
Every star means something to you
It might be someone watching you
Someone special who you know
May be your foe
Easy come, easy go
You'll find a friend wherever you go
Stars far away look like glitter
Making its way here
A voice beneath you said...
'Go, go, far.'
I find a black hole
It's open too
I get really scared but

I wake up and I'm right next to you!
My puppy licks my mouth, then she runs, she runs.

Erin O'Mara
Wootton St Andrew's Primary School, Wootton

About The Eevee Sisters

In Pokémon Go there are the Eevee sisters
Don't you dare mess with them or you'll be dead
Vaporeon is awesome on health
It's also very excellent on stealth
Jolteon, she's the best! (In my opinion!)
She puts all other Pokémon to rest
Flareon's the master of fire
Don't get burnt up in her desire
Espeon's the psychic master
She'll be your best friend
She'll destroy anything that's poisonous
But against darkness... wham! Your best friend's gone
Umbreon's the darkness master
Ghosties beware! Umbreon's here
Now go find the Eevee sisters
And you'll rule the world! Yeah!

Thomas Potter (11)
Wootton St Andrew's Primary School, Wootton

The Unicorn Sea Monsters

The unicorn sea monsters swimming in the sea
Not waiting to be caught swimming happily
The big Red Beard Pirate waiting for his fame
Trying to catch the unicorn beast again and again and again

All of a sudden a baby monster gets pulled up
For its fins all caught
And it makes Red Beard's day

He sails back home to collect his reward
When he gets back he only gives a push away
You hurt an endangered species of life
Now you can't come into town today

Poor Red Beard Pirate, he didn't know
He's out of town for one whole day
Looks like he will have to find fame another day

Jessica Hutson
Wootton St Andrew's Primary School, Wootton

Super Jack

S uddenly I saw some bubbling green lava and rocky ground
U nder the rough dirty ground
P atiently I waited for the bubbling green lava to overflow at the
E nd of the lost worlds! In the middle of the lost world
R andomly this alien appeared and he was my friend Leon and he
H ad a thought that there was a bad guy but he appeared from
E arth, but he looked like a burnt gingerbread man but the battle was
R idiculous because we just threw green lava at each other but
O ther than that, he was at the edge so I pushed his feet off, then he fell off.

Jack Clark (9)
Wootton St Andrew's Primary School, Wootton

Once Upon A Dream

O h no, I had a dream that I saw a fairy
N o this can't be happening to me, I'm sure it was a dream
C andy is waving all around
E nding with a flash

U nicorn popped out and scared me
P ears and apples, apples and pears
O n a rainy day
N othing can stop me because I can solve your problems right away

A nd how do you solve your problems?

D ream the night away
R ummaging around to see what's there
E ating what is left
A round you will find
M agic everywhere.

Amelia Rose Keir (9)
Wootton St Andrew's Primary School, Wootton

Lost In A Dream

L ost in the clouds
O ver everyone in town
S cared and lost I am
T ime goes by and the sky is dark blue

I n the darkness I hear a peculiar noise
N o one is here, no one can save me, I have to do this alone

A clown! A monster! Shooting high into the sky

D are I go closer or will I get eaten?
R eady for anything but not this!
E veryone was so loud they could hear me, until out of nowhere...
A wizard appeared beside me and helped me home
M um, Dad, I'm home again.

Darcey Skelton (10)
Wootton St Andrew's Primary School, Wootton

Night Night

N othing has prepared me for this strange land
I n fact I was not half ready
G oing forward as nervous as can be
H iking up and up a mountain
T hen out of nowhere a unicorn came and said,
'Follow me,' I followed

N ine minutes later we were in Unicorn Land
I t was as purple as a galaxy. It was
G alaxy World, it was wonderful
H ow did I get here? I am in a dream
T hen I woke up as fast as a 700mph car.

Esmé Burbidge (8)
Wootton St Andrew's Primary School, Wootton

My Shoes

My shoes help you skip queues
They are mind control
But don't go on a patrol

My shoes fly but go very high
You wear them on your feet
They have lots of heat

My shoes go upside down
But some people wear very cosy gowns
My shoes will never fall
Just like my very bouncy ball
My shoes go faster than the speed of sound
But could they go faster than a greyhound?

Oliver Armstrong (10)
Wootton St Andrew's Primary School, Wootton

I Went To Mars!

I went to Mars
There were bright stars
I saw a rocket race
They were going at a tremendous pace

On Mars
Some people play guitars
What a mission I had
Especially when I met my foe

You in USA
Wish you could be up here every day
Although you have to pay

Living up here is a dream
Except when you're eighteen.

Lily Dannatt
Wootton St Andrew's Primary School, Wootton

A Bus Trip To The Moon

D reaming can do anything like a bus taking you to the moon
R emembering not to say, 'Will we be there soon?'
E very day is fun when travelling in the air
A nything could happen, you might fall out and fly back in
M aybe everyone will be there, the Queen might be too!

Gracie O'Mara (10)
Wootton St Andrew's Primary School, Wootton

Queen

- **Q** uacking along the street
- **U** and your friend went to sleep
- **E** ven though the sun is blazing hot an
- **E** lephant rocked up with a pot
- **N** obody knew why an elephant rocked up with a pot, it gave them a fright and a shock.

Kurtis Filby (11)
Wootton St Andrew's Primary School, Wootton

YoungWriters
Est.1991

YOUNG WRITERS INFORMATION

We hope you have enjoyed reading this book – and that you will continue to in the coming years.

If you're a young writer who enjoys reading and creative writing, or the parent of an enthusiastic poet or story writer, do visit our website **www.youngwriters.co.uk**. Here you will find free competitions, workshops and games, as well as recommended reads, a poetry glossary and our blog.

If you would like to order further copies of this book, or any of our other titles, then please give us a call or visit **www.youngwriters.co.uk**.

Young Writers
Remus House
Coltsfoot Drive
Peterborough
PE2 9BF
(01733) 890066
info@youngwriters.co.uk